Dewdrops of Amrit

Poems that see my sea

Deepak Prasad

BookLeaf
Publishing

India | USA | UK

Made with ♥ on the BookLeaf Publishing Platform
www.bookleafpub.in
www.bookleafpub.com

Dedicated

To my

Ammamma & Muthacha

Acknowledgement

I am deeply grateful to:

My family, for their unwavering love and support, even when my journeys took me far from home.

The ocean, for her constant presence, wisdom, and inspiration, which has shaped me in ways I am still discovering.

My teachers, who instilled in me a love for words and the courage to express myself.

My friends on land and sea, who shared stories, laughter, and tears with me, and kept me grounded.

BookLeaf Publishing, for challenging me to pen down my thoughts in English after a long gap, for believing in my work and for cheerfully going back to the drawing board time and again to redesign the cover pages, to re-edit the illustrations, providing me with the valuable insights and working tirelessly to bring my ideas into life.

To Aisola sir, for agreeing to review my book in the last moment and bless me with his kindness and wisdom.

And to my dear friend, companion and confidant, who has been the single most inspiring and encouraging presence in my writing journey. Your unwavering faith in me and my words has meant the world; may this book be a testament to the power of your love and support.

Preface

The oceans have been my companion, my confidant, and my catalyst. They took me away from the familiarity of my life, giving me a bird's eye view from afar – and sometimes, no view at all, strikingly similar to the Maya that engulfs us in this cosmic ocean. In the vast expanse of the sea, I found myself lost and found, again and again.

As I navigated the waves, new perspectives on life, love, and purpose unravelled before me. The distance from my roots allowed me to re-evaluate what truly matters, understand the necessity to hold on to my roots and gave me a glimpse into the paradox of life, i.e., complete embracement & absolute detachment is one and the same.

These poems, like the waves of the ocean, just came to me. They're a reflection of my love for family, my passion for serving humanity, and my quest for meaning. They're not something I tried to create out of my intellect or as a result of my conquest for innovation. They are a creation of their own, I just happened to be on their path.

Through these verses, I invite you to join me on this journey of self-discovery, to ride the waves of life with me, and to find solace in the words that have been my anchor.

May these poems be a reminder that even in the most turbulent of times, there is beauty to be found, and that the sea of life is always worth exploring – even when it takes us far from shore.

Review

"DEEPAK Prasad's Rhymes of the Modern Mariner are the true and honest musings of a family man with strong roots on Land and yet adrift at sea.

His poems cover a wide range of subjects from strong family bonds to nature of fast changing communication technology to reflections on Life and its true nature and purpose. There is the sense of loss and time wasted mingling with a sense of hope. Life at sea can be very lonely and challenging and brings out facets of a personality that life on terra firma may not. The perspective is of endless open spaces with an ever receding horizon. It is emptiness all around and one seeks "Poorna" plenitude in that emptiness, both being two sides of the same coin. There is the joy of being at sea, pun intended and the expectation of getting back home to loving , welcoming arms.

Humans are complex and sailors perhaps more so by the very nature of their lives. No fixed home but a perpetual longing for home and hearth. Plenty of wanderlust and parallely a desire for firm roots and solidity. Love for shifting sands and moving boards and yet a desire for a firm footing. All this comes through in Deepak's poems.

I congratulate him for this excellent effort and wish his readers a happy cruise."

Ambassador Ravi Shankar Aisola IFS(Retd.)

Contents

The Price of Pursuit

For getting a better life, we race
Forgetting our family time
Forgetting that they never had you there
For getting their sight, we sit and stare

For getting a glimpse of their lovely face
Forgetting the memories we never had in
place
For getting a moment to share and care
Forgetting that it is too late and despair

For getting them a better life, we did roam
Forgetting my family, my heart's home
Forgetting their moments that would never
repeat
For getting them convenient and ever upbeat

For getting them educated and fine
Forgetting that we'd be left behind
For getting them degrees and a life of ease
Forgetting the love that brought me to my
knees

For getting food, but not feasts to share
Forgetting the memories we once spare
For getting a room, but not a home
Forgetting the love that we once called our
own

For getting a better future, we worked
Forgetting that present that we shirked
For getting old, we're now confined
Forgetting the joy we could've enshrined

For getting us meals and pills on time
Forgetting we yearn for their look onetime
For getting what did we forget our life
Forgetting what we forgot was our life.

A Ship & her Sailor

As you leave my helm, dear sailor true,
Your watch's ended, your tenure through.
I'll miss your firm hand on telegraph,
Guiding me full ahead, with your sweet laugh.

We've sailed through GoA and many a pirate's
nest,
Rough Bay of Biscay and calm Pacific's crest.
Snow falls, sand storms & nights with sun so
bright,
TRS avoidance, through the dark of night.

PSC inspections, we've cleared with pride,
ISPS protocols, our security's guide.
Safety meetings, and monthly drills myriad,
De-rusting, chipping, and hydro blasting
period.

Ballasting, and bunkering, we've done with
care,
Piston pull, and liner job, with precision fair.
Now it's time for your sign-off, leave me, go
elsewhere
Unsure our paths will ever cross, isn't it
unfair?

So if you hear a distress call, in the dark of
night,
Or a Pan-Pan message discern, that's my
beacon light.
My EPIRB will echo your name through the
deep blue sea,
My SART shall make 12 dot blips and guide
you back to me.

As my anchors are aweigh, my heart becomes
heavy,
As you climb down the gangway, my mind
feels chevy.
You've been my Polaris, guiding me so far,
From now on, my Pelorus will search you
near and far.

The sea is still, its waves so calm
But can't you see, my heart's in storm
The horizon is bright, with a sky so clear
Without you in sight, they blur, despair

Memoirs of our adventures will be sung till
the oceans dry,
May fair winds lead you home my friend,
farewell for now, aye aye!

My Mother - The Teacher

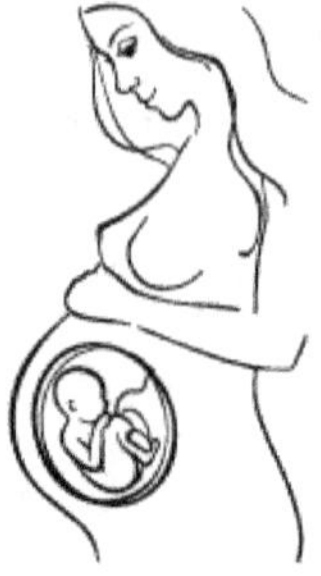

My mom, a teacher, so fine and so dear,
With a heart full of passion, and a spirit so
clear.
She taught with dedication, day after day,
Aiming for perfection, a teacher's cliché.

With marks and grades, she'd keep score,
But deep down her love would outpour.
She'd nag and remind me to sit and study
hard
For nothing short of a centum she wants on
my scorecard.

I remember her zeal, her drive and her might,
Pushing me to succeed, with all her light.
She'd ask where I lost that one mark, with a
grin,
All those teacher's kids—oh dear, you do
know what I mean.

My mom, a teacher, an HM so true,
Abundance of love, unless exams are due.
So here's to my mom, with a heart full of gold,
A treasure so precious, forever to hold!
A nectar so delicious like her masterpiece
stew
A blessing so priceless, ubiquitous, so true.

Mi Padre

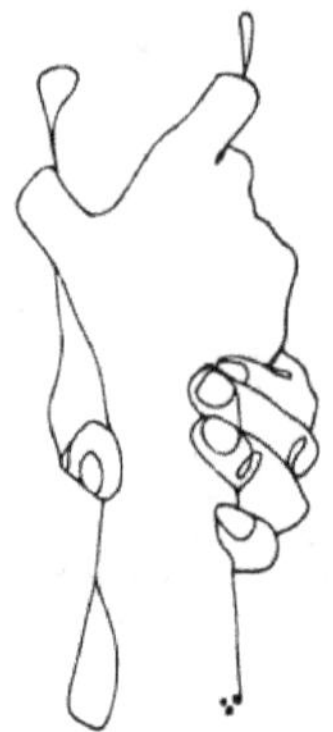

Whenas a youth, I knew my sire's affection
true,
Yet, as a father now, I see thine depths anew
Of sacrifice and care, of guidance and might,
The boundless love thou bore, in endless,
shining light

In precious moments, I do feel thy love's pure
fire
A depth I never knew, though I did e'er aspire
To thank thee more, to cherish every fleeting
hour
And in thy love, find solace, in its endless
power

Now, as a father, I do taste life's sweetest
delight
In joyful bliss, my heart doth sing with love's
pure light
Yet, with all my heart, I wish to be reborn
anew
As thy dear son, dear father, if fate's threads I
could renew.

Dilemma

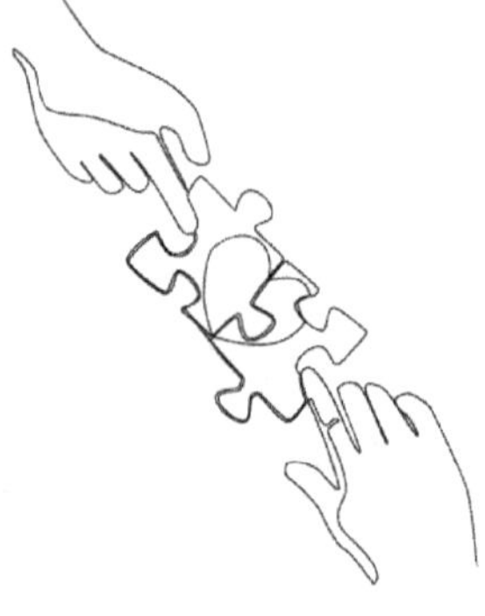

When you realize that the best thing you did
to yourself
was the worst thing you did to someone
or that the worst thing you did to yourself
was the best thing you did to someone
or if the first thought was right
or was it the last which was correct..
or if it would ever matter which was correct
for which you doubt if you could ever correct
or when the best thought in your mind
gives you the worst nightmare
or when the worst thought in your mind
is, you can't stop thinking of doing something
when you know for sure all you can do is
nothing

and then you doubt if all that has been done
is the same thing
and then you plead if you could stop this
thing
or at least stop thinking of the thing that you
want to think the least
when you keep thinking the same thing to see
if there is a way to prevent this thing
and then the things that you think brings you
back to the same thing
where you started thinking
or maybe where your thinking stopped!

Re-quest

When I see the lazy sun refusing to rest,
I forget how fast the time goes for the rest.
then I feel how far has my quest,
taken me from the hand that held my wrist.

When I see the sleepy albatross gliding to
west,
I forget in what a rush are the rest.
then I feel how far has my quest,
taken me from the land I like the best.

When I see the sky turn saffron at the dusk.
mind forgets that memories never rust.
then I feel how fine has this test,
shown me now all that I love the most.

Ode of the Unseen

O, fairest speck of dust, unseen by mortal
sight,
How oft thy absence doth unleash a tempest's
might.
A gentle zephyr, kind whisper in the air,
can fill thy heart with joy beyond compare.

A tiny seed, planted in the fertile soil,
Doth grow into a tree, a wonder to beguile.
A single word, spoken in kindness, true,
Can mend a broken heart, make spirits anew.

Why do we overlook the small and slight,
Until 'tis gone, and we're plunged in night.
Why do we not cherish every little thing
that brings us joy, a sweet, celestial spring.

Smallest things in might and power, do lie
To shape thy lives, hour to hour, sky high.
Let us embrace the small, tiny, easy things as
lief
For in them lie keys to foison of bliss in life.

Want

What do I have to do, to do what I want?
If I have to do what you want
To get to do what I want
Will that count as I got to do what I want
'cos I never wanted to do what you want!

When would I get to do what I want?
If I have to wait as much as you want
To get to do what I want
Will that count as I got to do what I want
'cos I never got to do it when I want!

How could I get to do what I want?
If how I want to do what I want
Had to be how you want
Will that count as I got to do what I want
'cos I never got to do it how I want!

Why can't I just do what I want?
Why does what I want have to be what you
want
So that you would even grant me to even
want what I want
Why is it such a crime to even want?

A Sailor's Dawn

Breaking dawn marks the rays of hope,
Breaking down everyday's mope,
Making drown our troubles we cope,
Staking our own life, we arise atop.

Finding our way, through darkness we grope,
Racing against time, with a frantic lope,
Washing away fears, with a gentle soap,
Drowning our sorrows, until we tope.

Fighting storms, we keep on scope,
Making waves, our spirit's rope,
Taking risks, our hearts elope,
Making dreams, our souls cope.

The Puzzling Purpose

Am I the body, vessel of clay?
Or mind, a spirit, a vibrant ray?
Where does my essence truly reside?
Within this form, or far and wide?

My mind can wander, to a distant land,
While my body rests upon the sand.
How can this be, if they are one?
A puzzle of self, forever spun.

Am I defined by feelings deep?
Or thoughts that race, and never sleep?
Either path will lead to the same,
Unless I conform, a puppet's game.

To solve this riddle, a lifetime's quest,
Yet few explore, where they will rest.
A tragic truth, a wasted chance,
To find oneself, a cosmic dance.

Value

Nothing but that matters the most
Until you get to achieve,
Missing the fact that it's all but lost
Perplexed, you sit & grieve,
Puzzling in between is the fact
Why can't we perceive.

A tree and her sapling

Mamma, Mamma, who are these trouts?
why they pluck your fruits, don't they have
roots?

oh dear child, they are our crop, humans
denote
we feed them with fruits and they have no
roots

we take their breath and make these sweet
fruits
we give them oxygen to sustain and sprout

they wander and reap and ripe and perish
and wither in this soil for us to cherish
22

oh dear child, they know not the truth
chimeric of ruling the planet with brute.

Ikigai

One should chase purpose, not just grades'
might
Loading passion, not just knowledge in sight
Seeking meaning, not just marks to display
Living life fully, every single day

Embracing life's gentle, guiding light
Finding joy in work, and balance in sight
Not just a job, but a life that's true
Living with purpose, that's what we should
do.

Give & Receive

No matter what, a closed palm can't receive.
Open your heart and your palm to give,
& you just can't believe how much you'll
receive.
'Cos all that you reave, death will bereave,
Except what you achieve for the love & care
you give.

Liberated

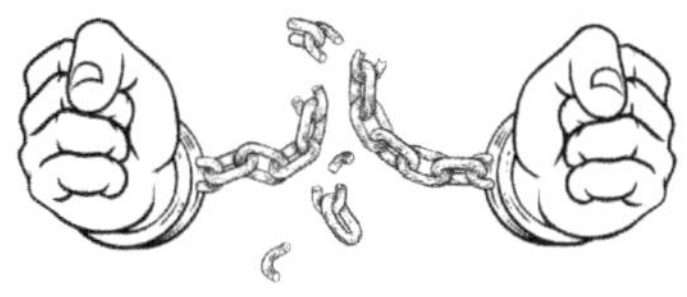

This World's a whirlpool, Life's caught in this
flood.
But I can't take it cool; it's not in my blood.

Working like a tool, to fetch daily bread.
Looking like a fool, it's better to be dead.

Sweating at the school, bookworm
knucklehead.
Gulping like a cesspool, well-read but misled.

Earning cash & drool, working even in bed.
Weeping on barstool, caring for love instead.

Wasting life like a fool, doing no one no good.
Wetting pants with stool, till breath leaves
you dead.

Swimming in this pool, I'm drowning till bed.
Fighting for my soul, heading where my mind
led.

You should do it too, let's get the word spread.
It ain't no taboo, it's your birthright instead.

Let us end this dule, let's not get wasted.
Let our hearts rule, let's get liberated.

REgain

REwind the time
REnew your prime
REfuel the spirit
REverse the inhibit
REturn to nature
REtune your aperture
REfine the mind
REmind to be kind
REpair the despair
REfresh your flair
RElive your way
REpeat everyday

<u>W</u> is the real <u>L</u>

When do you know the meaning of life?
when you meet someone who loves your life,

Even in truce and same way in strife,
Even way more than her very own life!

When Everything in your life becomes her,
When every beat of your heart chants her
name,

When every breath you take seeks her scent,
When everywhere you look seeks her sight,

When everyone in the world calls her your
wife.
Then you'll know the truth that she is your
life.

Ma Bro

Hey Ani, my lil bro, I'm writing this for you
Nine years younger, but our bond's still true
I left for the sea, you were just a seed
Growing up fast, like a weed, indeed.

I'd come back home, and you'd doubled in size
From baby bro to homie, our bond realized
We shared the same interests, same passions
too
Photography, riding, traveling—our dreams
came true.

But then you found a new love, a motherly
affection true
For my wife, who cares for you, like a mom,
through and through
Then came our little bundle, spreading joy
and glee
Mom and Dad regained their childhood, and
you were jumping with spree.

Yo, champ chase your dreams, PhD plant
biotech
In Australia, the last continent for me to
check
I missed it as a sailor, but now achieved it
through you
Watching you I'm beaming with pride, in
every step, I'm beside you.

We'll plan our trips, bike rides and hikes and
adventures to do
Pan India, ride on our motorbikes, reach
Kardungla too
Kailash trek, the prime divine, bro we ought
to do,
Lord Shiva, keep watching; we're coming for
you.

But now the distance stretches far,
still, in my heart, you're never too far.
My bro, my friend, together we've found,
a bond that's strong, a friendship profound.

So here's to my bro, my partner, let it rhyme
We'll ride together, in time, in perfect crime
Our bond's a flame, that burns bright and free
A love that's strong, and forever we'll be.

Twilight

When the bright eternal source of light,
peeps out of the mist to wish good night,

for those who sail over the oceans' might,
is it delight, the plight or trite twilight?

Insight or hindsight, there isn't slight despite,
for fight we shall, all day, all night,

You just be alight,
sleep tight, good night.

It's Now / Never

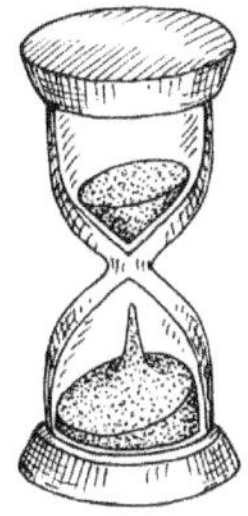

In the realm of time, only one truth shines
bright
This moment, now, where life takes flight
Don't dwell on the past, let go of the pain
Nor worry about the future, its path unseen

For this moment, right here, is your future's
stage
What you do now paves the way, turns the
page
And when it's gone, it becomes your past
So live it well, and it will forever last

Bring your mind to the present, let go of fear
Stop worrying about what's yet to appear
For in this moment, your future is born
Nurture it well, and it will forever bloom

Script your destiny, with every breath you
take
In this moment, let your true self awake
So live it fully, with heart and soul
For this moment, now, is your ultimate goal.

A letter to recall

In days of yore, the postman's bell would ring
A symbol of love, a letter to bring

From distant lands, a message so dear
A wait so long, a joy so clear

Then came the land phone, a trunk call's
sound
Not just for one house, but a hundred others
around

Kids would run, with feet so fast
To call a neighbour, who'd rush at last

To hear the voice, that they loved so true
A rare delight, for a community anew

Pagers arrived, with emergency's might
A digital telegram, shining bright

Mobile phones, a connection so true
A range so humble, a heart so new

Video calls, group calls, VR and many more
A world so connected, yet decaying at its core

While sitting side by side, yet searching far
away
tapping on the wedge that's drifting them
astray

Necessity to connect, drove innovation's fire
Now we're all but lost, in a digital desire.

What a cycle

Corruption's subtle creep,
Like salt in water, dark and deep,
Seeps into the soul, a slow poison's sway,
Tainting every drop, day by day.

Each drop protests with righteous tone,
"I'm pure, the sea's corruption's throne,"
But given chance to take a shortcut's way,
Each drop succumbs to corruption's sway.

Together they form a salty sea,
A collective corruption, for all to see,
A toxic tide that's hard to stem,
A poison, a wound, persistent harm.

At death's door, like evaporation's rise,
The soul departs, leaving corruption's
disguise,
In birth's pure rain, we start anew,
Unknowing of corruption, with a heart so
true.

But as we tread, the path grows worn,
And compromise becomes the norm,
Justifying each step, each choice we make,
Between right and wrong, the thin line fade.

Why can't we resist the subtle sweat,
And work towards the day when sea turns
sweet.
When integrity prevails, and corruption
retreats
The ocean turns pure, with every drop that
meets.

Many gazillion drops make the ocean wide,
Let's sweeten the ocean, drop by drop, with
pride.
Then corruption's grip will slowly fade,
And the ocean's heart will be pure and made.

Time fly's

In a forgotten corner, where shadows lie
A rotting apple core, became my birthplace
high

I emerged from the decay, with life's spark
aglow
A tiny, wriggling thing, destined to grow

I grew and learned, with each passing hour
Mastering wings, in my tiny flower

I made some friends, who danced with glee
Together we'd soar, wild and free

We'd explore the world, with curious eyes
Sipping sweetness, from sun-kissed surprise

I found my love, in a warm summer breeze
We'd dance and flutter, with tender ease

We built a life, in a cozy little nest
And soon our babies, would be at their best

But life is short, and time flies by fast
I grew old quickly, my wings wouldn't last

I looked back on life, with a grateful heart
For every moment, we played our part

And as I lay, in my final rest
I thought of humans, and their self-imposed
test

They think their lives, are long and grand
But like mine, they're short, in this busy land

So don't be pathetic, don't waste your time
Start living, start giving, make your mark
shine

Help other lives, spread love and kindness too
For life is short, but its impact can shine
through

At least I flew, with the wind beneath
And lived my life, with no regrets or breath

So take a cue, from my fleeting light
And make the most, of your precious life

Fear is your Fire

Butterflies flutter, a fluttery sight,
A racing heart, a thrilling delight.
Adrenaline surges, a wild, giddy thrill,
Fear and excitement, side by side, still.

One is a passenger, a helpless ride,
Fear takes the wheel, a frightening guide.
The other, a driver, in full control,
Excitement takes charge, a soaring soul.

So let's grab the helm, with a steady hand,
And turn fear's engine to a fiery band.
For in the heart, where passions ignite,
Fear can be fuel, a guiding light.

Destiny

Desire, a driving force, compels our way,

Even paths we'd rather avoid, we stray.

Sometimes desires clash with nature's might,

Then desires become a reactive fight.

In this endless cycle, trapped we roam,

Never finding peace, forever alone.

Yielding to fate, we blame the stars above,

Despair consumes, devoid of hope or love.
Emancipate yourself, take charge and choose,
Set your desires, let your spirit ooze.
The drive within, a powerful, guiding light,
Inspires actions, makes it feel just right.
No matter what life throws, you'll stand so
tall,
Your spirit soaring up, answering the call.

Don't let desires falter, don't give in,
Embrace the challenge, let your spirit win.
Set a destiny, a grand, ambitious goal,
Take control of life, let your spirit stroll.
Inspire yourself, let your passion burn,
Never let life's storms your spirit turn.
Your destiny is yours, to shape and mould,
A tale you write yourself, is the destiny to be
told.

Grow up to Childhood

Why do we toil, and why do we strive?
For jobs and for wealth, we're all alive.
We seek sustenance, medicine, and more,
Yet life's essence, perhaps, lies in store.

Time, a fleeting gift, a precious span,
Is filled with purpose, a grand human plan.
We immerse ourselves, find joy and delight,
In moments of bliss, so pure and bright.

Like children who play, with hearts full of
glee,
No worries or cares, wild and free.
Why can't we linger, in that childlike state,
And find solace, before it's too late?

Time, swift or slow, depends on our state,
It flies; immersed in joy, a fleeting mate.
But when we reflect, the hours stretch and
creep,
A testament to how our feelings keep.

Unhappiness drags, a heavy, leaden weight,
Though eons may pass, life's story's brief and
late.
Shaped by choice, our feelings, not
circumstance,
Can dictate how we feel, a life's romance.

So grow and mature, take charge, and invest,
Live a life of impact, a noble quest.
Control your feelings, rise above the fray,
Be a child at heart, in a vibrant way.

Seek excitement, joy, and endless glee,
Unburdened by sorrow, wild and free.
A childlike spirit, resilient and strong,
Can weather life's storms, and make them
belong.

Apology

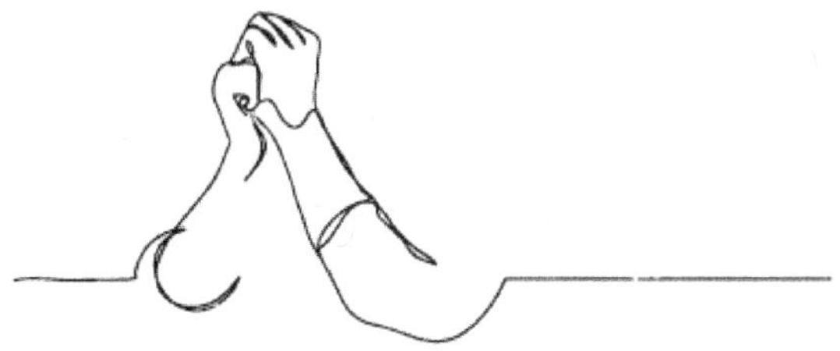

I'm sorry for all those that I ever did
I'm sorry for all those that I never did
I'm sorry for all those that I ever said
I'm sorry for all those that I never said
I'm sorry for what I did which I never said
I'm sorry for that I said which I never did
I'm sorry for all those times I was never there
I'm sorry for not being there when you want
me near
I'm sorry for not watching you when you
want me to
I'm sorry for not seeing you when you wish
me to
I'm sorry for not saying all that I should have
said
I'm sorry for not listening all those you had
said

I'm sorry for all those which I did as pleased
I'm sorry for all those which left you
displeased
I'm sorry for all wrongs that I did knowingly
I'm sorry for all I had done unknowingly
I'm sorry for suing you for my loss of dream
I'm sorry for not pursuing it with full extreme
I'm sorry for all those times I forgot to live
I'm sorry for all those times when I didn't
believe
I'm sorry for those kisses that I never return
I'm sorry for those moments that I wish
would return
I'm sorry for all that I have ever written
I'm sorry for not writing those I should have
written
I'm sorry for making you feel I don't
understand
I'm sorry for taking so long to make my own
stand
I'm sorry for not saying so when I really
meant
I'm sorry for not saying sorry till this
moment.

The forgotten roar

In days of yore, before the history's birth,
A forest thrived, 'neath mountains' mighty
mirth,
And oceans vast, where creatures roamed
free,
A haven for all, in cosmic harmony.

Lions, tigers, panthers, elephants did stride,
Deers, yaks, monkeys, and oxen, side by side,
Peacocks spread their plumes, serpents
slithered by,
Eagles soared, around the globe, sharing the
forest's sigh.

Falcons came, camels too, seeking fruits to
share,
Trade prospered with wine and wise, as the
world gazed in awe,
But wolves and packs, reached the forest's
shores with conquest in their eyes,
Trembling they fled, at the lions' roar, and
elephants' seismic stride.

Pigs snuck in, under night's dark shade,
Plundering roots, leaving squirrels afraid,
Lions and tigers chased them away, with a
mighty roar,
But pigs burrowed the rifts between, and
claimed lands galore.

Jackals came, with cunning guile,
Pitting pigs and lions, in a wicked smile,
Camels and cows, in dispute did stray,
As jackals gained control, and ruled the
forest's day.

Rifts grew wide, as animals did fight,
Some protested, others fled, in endless night,
One day the jackals aghast, left in all but
haste and plight,
leaving behind a forest divided, near and far
in sight.

Pigs were gifted a land of their own not one
but two in greed.
Yet some remained, and jackals too, preaching
their wicked creed,
Lion cubs howled, and so did tiger cubs too,
serpents shushed their snakelets hiss.

The forest was free, yet it seemed to grieve
Forgetting their nature, independent yet
suppressed,
Imprisoning themselves, and the forest's tales
repressed.

Oh, dear cubs, wake up, and roar with might,
Oh, mighty ox, moo loud, and shine with
light,
Oh, sapient serpent, hiss, and claim your
rightful place,
Oh, burly elephant, raise your tusks, and
show your noble face.

Let the forest's glory rise, once more,
Let the animals remember, their true nature's
score,
For in unity and strength, they'll find their
way,
To a brighter dawn, and a new shining day.

Break free from chains that bind your mind,
Shed lies that shroud your ancestors' prime,
Embrace the tales of your mighty past,
Unleash your true nature, and let it forever
last.

Namaste,

As I pen this note, I'm overwhelmed with a mix of emotions: excitement to share my journey, gratitude for your readership, and a childish eagerness to know your take on it.

I'm a navigator by profession, engineer by graduation, photographer, writer, rider, traveller, footballer, social servant and more by passion, a worshiping son, a loving husband, a caring and daring father, a friendly brother and a brotherly friend.

I'm extremely proud of my culture and tradition, at the same time I'm not ready to accept any custom as blind believer, instead challenging it by trying to study, based on its historic, scientific, physiological significance to differentiate the actual traditions from falsified superstitions.

One who strives to perform his meagre part to transform the world into a better place for everyone and to transform everyone for the betterment of the world.

This book is an effort to reflect my journey, my thoughts and my dreams within the limitations of the medium. I hope that it will inspire you to reflect on your own journey, to question the status quo, and to strive for a better world.
Thank you for joining me on this journey. I look forward to hearing your thoughts and feedback.

Sincerely

Deepak Prasad

Aiswarya, Old Village, Nemmara
Palakkad, Kerala, India-678 508
Capt.deepakprasad@gmail.com
+91 773 615 8334